Help Wanted Fathers, Apply in Person

Warren L. Baker Sr.

Cadmus Publishing
www.cadmuspublishing.com

Copyright © 2022 Warren L. Baker Sr.

Published by Cadmus Publishing
www.cadmuspublishing.com
Port Angeles, WA

ISBN: 978-1-63751-345-3

All rights reserved. Copyright under Berne Copyright Convention, Universal Copyright Convention, and Pan-American Copyright Convention. No part of this book may be reproduced, stored in a retrieval system, or transmitted in any form, or by any means, electronic, mechanical, photocopying, recording or otherwise, without prior permission of the author.

DEDICATION

This book is dedicated to the remembrance of my mother, Martha Baker, who, during the most challenging times of my life was my greatest role model. All of my life all I ever really wanted to do was to make her proud, she has truly been an inspiration in my life, even though now she is passed away and gone to be with the Lord.

This book is also dedicated to my son's, Warren Jr., Desmond, and my stepson Javario. You were the one's who gave me encouragement to write this book. To see that all three of you have grown up to be great young men is amazing. With all the odds you have had against you in my absence, you survived, and I know that it was through the grace of God, and I thank Him daily for being a Father to you all.

Introduction

This book is a preemptive attempt to introduce you to one of our greatest problems in the family, which is the absence of fathers from the home. This is a major epidemic in our American families and if left unchecked we will continue to lose our young men and young ladies to drugs, gangs, violence, prison, teenage pregnancy, runaways, and suicide.

Today, if you would ask the mothers, wives, sisters, daughters, and girlfriends about the whereabouts of the men in their lives, you would find that too many of them will say that they are either in or have just gotten out of jail or prison. Today, a large number of our young men are being gunned down on our streets, as well as many innocent victims to gangs and gun violence.

In this book, I share many of my experiences of incarceration. One of those experiences includes seeing a father and a son incarcerated together, as well as the high number of young men I see each day that come behind these prison walls who are from fatherless homes. I will also share with you a bit about my son's being raised in a fatherless home, and how they forgave me in my absence and how God has reconciled us together again.

I would like for this book to get the attention of fathers on how important it is for them to be in their children's lives. I believe we can put a dent in the negative statistics of the absences of fathers in the home. This book is a compilation of statistics, firsthand experiences, and observations that are intended to be a red flag that will hopefully raise some more awareness and concern about this crisis. Maybe, just maybe, we can collectively demand some attention be given to this, and possibly bring about a change to what is happening in our American homes as it concerns this epidemic of the absence of fathers in the home.

Table of Contents

Chapter One 1
Chapter Two: What inspired me to write this book 5
Chapter Three: Father Brings Discipline to Children 18
Chapter Four: The Need For More Praying Fathers 24
Chapter Five: The Scars of Yesterday 30
Chapter Six: Testimony Of My Father's Last Days 36
Chapter Seven: Becoming a Man 40
Chapter Eight: More Statistics on the Absence of Fathers in the Home ..48
Chapter Nine: When Children become Mothers and Fathers 53
Chapter Ten: Learning to Forgive 60
Chapter Eleven: The Mothers Role in the Absence of the Father 66
Chapter Twelve: Fathers and Mothers Working for the Betterment of their Children After a Divorce or Separation 71

Chapter One

As I was reading the daily newspaper, I ran across a section in the paper they call the "want ads," which was a classified advertisement for employment. It listed jobs that were available for hiring. During that time, while I was reading, my mind began to ponder on the throught as to what was one of the greatest needs that effects our children in the home. As I pondered, the thought came to me that one of these was the absence of fathers in the home.

I believe this thought came to me because I had previously read and heard many statistics on the absence of fathers in the home, but most of all, the thought came to me because I have sons who were young when I came to prison, and they were left fatherless. This topic came to me through reading the want ads section in the newspaper. "Help Wanted Fathers, Apply in Person." Well, before we begin, I want you to know that

I'm writing from behind prison walls. I just felt the need to be transparent with you before we start this journey.

I'm certainly not proud to be here nor am I proud to be writing from such a place as this prison, but I know that I cannot change the past. Neither of us has the power to do that, but I do have the ability to change my future. I am hoping that I can help some young man or woman change their future from coming, so they make the right decision and do not end up behind these prison walls. Believe me or not, but we have all got some kind of life experiences we have been through that other people could learn from, because we have all made bad choices at one time or another in life.

Failure is an event, not a person. In this life, we will all experience failure one way or another, but that failure does not define who we are. As for me, my setbacks are comebacks and that is where I stand with the writing of this book. It is a comeback because, I decided to use those failures and bad choices I have made in the past to redirect my future for better things such as fulfilling my God given purpose here on Earth. Being in prison is not God's will for me, nor any of you.

In 1 Corinthians 10:11, the Apostle Paul makes a profound statement. He says, "Now, all these things happened unto them as examples: and they are written for our admonition, upon whom the ends of the ages are come." The experiences of our forefathers and their failures are examples for our learning so that we do not repeat our forefathers' sins. This is my prayer and my wish, so that fathers do not experience the failures of their forefathers', and especially so that my son's do not experience my failures by repeating them.

There are two things in life that you can learn from. You can learn from others' mistakes, or you can make your own mistakes and learn from them. Believe me, it is better to learn from other people's mistakes and save yourself a lot of headaches, time, money, and sleepless nights. Take time out and learn from other people who have made bad choices at one time or another, so you will not find yourself walking in their footsteps. Just ask yourself this question, "Do I want my son or daughter repeating my failures and bad choices?" I believe that if you answer truthfully, your answer would be NO.

I wish and pray that this book will reach fathers beyond these prison walls and that it will motivate them to man-up and be the man that God has created them to be. Maybe, just maybe, we will be able to save a younger generation from coming to such a place as this "prison" and repeating our mistakes.

What statistics say about fatherless homes

Statistics state that 80% of all youth sitting in prison today grew up in a fatherless household. Statistics also say that 70% of high school dropouts come from fatherless homes and that 70% of juveniles in state operated institutions come from fatherless households. Believe me when I say that there are even more statistics about this that I have not quoted here.

Today there is mass incarceration of men in prison and many of these men who are incarcerated have left behind young children at home to be parented by a single parent. We have read the statistics of that child in the absence of their fathers. If American families are going to survive then fathers must get back to their rightful place, which is The Home.

Did you know that the United States of America has more people incarcerated than any other nation in the world, and that a large number of these men are fathers who are absent from the home? We have been known as one of the greatest superpower nations in the world, but it looks like we have become a superpower nation in locking men and women, boys and girls up in institutions. Today, many black people believe that prison here in America has become our modern-day plantations with the mass incarceration of black people.

Where is the money going?

Did you know that America spends more money on incarceration than on sending a young man or women to college? Believe it or not, prison here in America has become a BOOMING BUSINESS for many states and when one looks at private prisons and investors, it would seem like inmates have become high price stock cattle. Investors cannot wait to get their hands on some of the stocks, because they see a profit on their investment and it is sad to say, but business seems to be getting better by the moment. Just watch your news, they are tearing down the doors to get in prison, or at least, that is what it seems like, with the rise of crime on our streets due to drugs and gun violence.

Some would ask the question, where is the money going? It is going into someone's pocket, and it has becoming common practice.

Chapter Two

What Inspired Me to Write This Book

I wrote this book because around the year 2003, I had the experience of running across a father and son who were incarcerated together at the same prison that I was. I have heard of this before; I had never witnessed it first-hand. I had also heard that the son and the father were not speaking to each other. This was because the father had treated the son's mother badly and the father had abandoned them when the son was a baby to be raised by his mother alone.

I cannot even remember their faces. I can only remember that they were African American. But, my attention was not on their appearance, nor was it on their race. I can remember that they were black because I am a black man, and it is hard to forget someone when you are the same race as that person. My true attention was on them being father and son and locked up in prison together.

I believe that this touched my heart because I have son's and it would truly hurt my heart to see even one of them here with me behind these prison walls. That would be devasting to me. This is something I wish upon no one. I can truly say that this was the worst experience I have had in all my time here in prison so far, seeing a father and a son locked up together let alone not speaking to each other. That day, after gym call, I went back to my dorm and prayed for the father and his son that God would reconcile their relationship and heal their wounded hearts. I thanked God for putting Godly men and women in my son's lives, since I was not around to raise them.

Today, my sons are grown young men. They have turned out to be great young men and I am very proud of them. I remembered when I prayed in my county jail to God to take care of my son's and to place Godly influences in their lives. I cried out to God from the depths of my heart concerning the well being of my son's and he heard my cry, and I am appreciative to God for that. I am reminded of the words David said in Psalm 34:6, "this poor man cried, and the Lord heard him, and saved him out of all his troubles."

That day, I was that poor man crying out to God and He heard me. I also thank God that through the years I have been incarcerated, He has opened the line of communication between my sons and me. They have forgiven me, which is a milestone in any relationship if it is going to be reconciled. I truly thank God, because without Him, it would not have been possible. I realize that even in my unfaithfulness, He was faithful to me. Thank God that we serve a God of restoration and reconciliation. As Malachi 4:6 says, "He can turn the hearts of children unto their fathers." Even if the father has failed and made bad choices, God can turn it around if the father acknowledges his wrongs and then repent of them.

Today, there may be some of you who are reading this book at this present time and the devil has got you thinking that it is over with you being reconciled with your children or that the relationship can never be fixed. Well, I have news for you, the devil is a liar, and you should not be listening to the advice of a liar. The Bible says, with God all things are possible to him that believeth. Yes, there may be a lot of unforgiveness in your children's hearts towards your absence in their lives, but I want you to know that God can heal those wounded hearts.

I am a living witness to the power of God through restoration and reconciliation. As a matter of fact, one of the main reasons I've written this book is to help men be reconciled with their children, because it is not over until God says it is over.

My Prayer

I pray that God will do as Malachi 4:6 says, "turn the hearts of fathers back to their children and the hearts of the children to their father." If America's families are going to survive, something must change, and it must change by putting fathers back in their rightful place which is back in the home. Father's must learn the importance of them being in their children's lives.

I am not trying to preach to you, believe me, but if preaching to you is going to get you back in your rightful place, well, I am going to at least try. Perhaps you will listen to someone who has been there. It has been said that if you keep on doing the same thing looking for different results, then that is a form of insanity. Insanity is a form of mental illness, and if men keep on leaving home and not fulfilling their responsibility as father's, thinking that all is well in their absence, which is a form of insanity also, because we have read the statistics and they are devastating.

New arrivals are transferred in the prison that I am at two days a week. I see fathers, son, husband, uncles, cousins and even grandfathers every single week come here behind these prison walls. It grieves me to my heart because most of these men are fathers.

The New Face of Our American Streets

Have you watched the news lately? Well, with the rise of gang violence, it seems like the face of our American streets is young men who have gone wild. The million-dollar question is: Where are the fathers of these young men who are terrorizing our streets? There seems to be no positive mentors in their lives and that is because these young men or boys who make our news are byproducts of fatherless homes. Many turn to gangs because they want to be accepted, and then they turn to crime and drugs because these are the things that usually go with that lifestyle.

Today, many neighborhoods are being destroyed and innocent lives have been taken due to gun violence. Gun violence appears to be getting worse more than it is getting better these days. Many have asked the question, "when is this all going to stop?" That is the million-dollar question. One thing I believe is that if we get fathers back to their rightful place which is the home, then we can put a dent in the negative statistics.

I also believe that Ephesians 6:1-4 makes it plain about the responsibility of the parents in their children's lives. I know that we have all heard the quote about it taking a village to raise a child, but I do not see the word village in this scripture. The Apostle Paul is instructing parents in this scripture to raise their children. He is not instructing the village to raise the parent's children. The problem now is that too many villages have been raising our children and they are out of control. It is time that we fulfill our responsibility as parents and raise our own children. We must stop trying to push them off on somebody else. I guess the village has to raise them if we don't.

I'm living proof that all things will work together for good to those who love God and are called according to His purpose.

The Charge of A Father to His Son on His Death Bed

Now, let us take a look at a man named David. Yes, that's right. King David who was the father of Solomon. In 1 Kings 2:1-4, David gives a charge to his son Solomon while David is on his death bed. "Now, the days of David drew near that he should die, and he gave a charge to Solomon his son. 'I am about to go the way of all the earth." (1 Kings 2:1-2). David was talking about his grave and his death. "Be strong, therefore, and prove yourself a man, and keep the charge of the Lord your God to walk in His ways, to keep His statues, His commandments, His judgements, and His testimonies as it is written in the law of Moses, that you may prosper in all that you do and wherever you turn, that the Lord may fulfill his word which He spoke concerning me," (1 Kings 2:3-4). David told Solomon that if your sons take heed to their ways, to walk before me in truth with all their heart and with all their soul, that man would not lack a King on the throne of Israel.

David did not want to leave before he had instructed his son concerning the things of God. We too must be concerned about our children fulfilling God's will in their lives. Today, many fathers have failed in instructing their children concerning the instructions of God. It is sad to say, but many mothers have been filling the gap of doing what the father should have been doing in the lives of their children. I witnessed this firsthand because my mother was the Godly influence in our home.

Thank God for godly mothers and grandmothers, grandfathers, foster parents, single dads, and mentors. I salute you all for taking the time to make an impact in some child's life. No, not every father is a deadbeat dad. Thank God also for fathers that stick it out and raise their children no matter how hard it gets. I applaud every father out there including those who have gotten a divorce but have not divorced his children but instead continued to be active in his children's lives no matter what.

Solomon did prosper and he became the richest and wisest man on the earth, but through disobedience, he allowed his wives to turn his heart from the Lord. Just read Kings 11:1-3. It's sad to say, but it seems like his lust overrode his wisdom.

Man-Up

Help Wanted Father's, Apply in Person is pleading with you fathers to man-up and be Men. Your children's futures depend on you. You have just read the statistics of the fatherless homes at the beginning of this book. Man-up is to stand up and take full responsibility to raise your children in the admonition and the fear of the Lord. Did you know that your children are a gift to you from God?

Psalms 127:3 states, "Behold, children are a heritage from the Lord. The fruit of the womb is his reward." Heritage is something that is passed down from preceding generations. Now, believe me or not, we all have one Father and that is God. Your children are a gift from God to you. Paul says in 1 Corinthians 4:2, "Moreover it is required in stewards that one be found faithful." Now, this alone let me know that God is holding parents accountable in how they raise His children. Parents are stewards of God's children.

I am a witness to the truth of the statistic that states that about 80% of youths sitting in prison grew up in fatherless homes. I see a large portion of these numbers every single day. It grieves me to my heart, because most of these young men are 18 to 25 years of age and are often times already affiliated with gangs in prison. If a young man who is 18 years of age is not affiliated with a gang upon entering prison, it is certain that through peer pressure, the need for protection and peer pressure that they will usually give in and join a gang in prison. Man-up is simply being a man physically, emotionally, and spiritually in the lives of your children.

Rapp Mentorship Group

Back in 2013 when I was in the faith-based program as a character coach. I had a burden on my heart to start a mentor's group for 18- to 30-year-old young men. There was another brother there who had the same burden as I had for these young men. We gathered and we organized a mentoring group called Rapp.

We started to meet once a week with the guys. Our goals were not to preach to them. We did have godly principles, and as a matter of fact our foundation scripture was taken from Proverbs 17:17 which says, "A friend loves at all times, and a brother is born for adversity." The guys who were members of the group already knew us and our character. We had already gained their trust and they knew that we really cared about them leaving prison and never returning.

Here is one thing that I have learned about young men today. It's hard to get their attention, but when you do, you have gotten it and they will follow you anywhere. When I look into one of those guys eyes, it is as though I'm looking into the eyes of my own son. They knew we really cared about them getting out of prison and wanting them to fulfill their God given purpose. We assured them that prison was not their future and God had a purpose for their lives and it was not prison.

We let them know that they were here because of bad choices. They were very real when they talked. One thing about young men is, they keep it real. We talk about things that they have dealt with daily behind these prison walls. We also talk about the stress of being locked up away from family and friends. We even talk about dealing with your bunkmate, because you share a limited amount of space together, above or under you. We agreed to confidentiality when one shares something personal in the group. If we heard that someone in the group talked to another person outside of the group concerning what someone shared in the group, then that person will be asked to dismiss himself from the group at the next meeting.

If we wanted to reach these guys, we had to have total confidentiality in the group. People do not share their personal lives with just anyone, so when they do, it should be kept between those he shared those details with. At times, I had suggestions and at times, others also had suggestions. Sometimes, they just wanted to vent, and we would let them vent while we listened. We saw many burdens lifted from the shoulders of these young men who just wanted to be heard.

I remember one group meeting we had where I asked a few of the guys who it was that had impacted in the most positive way in their lives. Some said their mother, one said his dad. It was good to hear that, because you do not hear dads name called that much these days. Two of the guys said their grandmothers, and out of nowhere, one said, "You, Brother Baker." That time, I really thought, "WOW, did he really just say that?" Tears began to bubble up in my eyes when I heard that.

I guess, when people see you really care, you impact their lives. Isn't that surprising that I am in here in prison mentoring young men and showing them the love of a father. Remember, you can always be a mentor to someone, and you will be surprised who God leads your way. Today, I wish I could get fathers to listen to the cries of their sons and their daughters because children are hurting, and it seems like no one is listening. Gangs, drug dealers, pimps, prison are listening, and they are offering those children their hearts desires and the gangs are offering them loyalty.

Now, my heritage dictionary defines loyalty as a feeling or an attitude of devoted attachment and affection. The bottom line is this. If you do not show your son or daughter affection then believe me, the gangs and drugs dealers will. I heard the cries of my son when he wrote me to say that he wished I was there to tie his tie. Fathers, it's time to listen to the cries of your children, because if you do not then someone else will and who knows whose hands your children will turn up in.

A Letter From My Son, Desmond

I remember a letter I got from my youngest son, Desmond, when he was graduating from high school. He stated that he wished I could be there to tie his necktie. Can you believe this? Something so simple as tying his necktie was what he wanted me to do, but due to my circumstances, I could not fulfill my son's only request because I was locked up behind prison walls.

Boy, that letter brought tears to my eyes because it let me know how much I was missed and needed for something as simply as tying my son's necktie. I believe that every father is missed by their children when he is absent from the home. My friend, you would be surprised how much your sons and daughters need you in their lives. I have written many letters and made many phones calls over the years just to talk to my son's and hear their voices over the phone. I even have had visits from one of my sons throughout the years, but nothing can replace being there with them. All those letters and phone calls were a substitute for my presence in the home, but thanks be to God for using those things to strengthen our relationship.

That is still not an excuse for me not being home raising my own sons.

The Responsibility of Fathers in the Home

In Ephesians 6:4, Paul speaks very profoundly about the responsibility of the father in the home. There are two commands here in Ephesians 6:4, the first being not to provoke your children to wrath. Avoid severity, anger, harshness, or cruelty. Cruel parents generally have bad children. Correct but do not punish as punishment is from a principle of revenge. Correction is from a principle of affection and concern. The second command to be found in this scripture is, "bring up children in the nurture and admonition of the Lord. Their mind is to be nourished with wholesome discipline and instruction which will bend them toward God and Christian living."

The word admonition in the American Heritage Dictionary is defined as meaning mild, kind, yet earnest, reproof, cautionary, advice or warning. A father should be kind and earnest in reproving his children. He should give advice and warning to his children, and this must be done through his love for them. My friend, the word of God is our manual for raising our children. It has all of the instruction that one needs if he is a father who wants to fulfill his responsibilities as a Godly father and one who fears God and wishes to raise his children up in fear and admonition of the Lord.

Today, there are all kinds of books out there with suggestions on raising your children and many of them have some good suggestions on that topic, but the best book out there is the Word of God, which is the Bible. It gives you Godly principal in raising your children. Remember when I told you that you are stewards of your children? Well, if we are stewards, then we need counsel from their original Father, which is God. Believe it or not, He wrote a book on how to raise His children and gave it to us and it is called the Word of God or the Bible.

He did not just give you a book on how to raise His children, but He also gave you a book on how He wants you to live your life here on earth. It is also the father's responsibility to demonstrate love in the home. Love is an expression of one's affection towards another. To embrace or care. Children need the affection shown to them by their parents. We all want to be loved, believe it or not. I have not met a person yet that did not want someone to love him or her. We find people striving for someone's love. It may be a wife from her husband or a husband from his wife, or a child from their parents.

The bottom line is that we all want to be loved by somebody and God is the one that places that desire in us, so you cannot run away from wanting to be loved. When a child is given love through his parents, it builds his confidence in life. His self-esteem is built, and he or she does not go seeking love in the wrong places and with the wrong people. They already feel valued and cared for and wanted.

When a child is not shown love in the home, he or she goes out searching and usually end up in the wrong places and with the wrong people such as gangs, drugs, sex, violence, and many more places. Sometimes, people will just use them up. God's kind of love is content. It is not boastful or proud, it behaves itself, it is not selfish, it does not have a short fuse, it does not keep score, it rejoices in truth, it can bear anything, it believes all things, hopes, endures, and it never fails.

When you get spare time just read how the Apostle Paul defines true love in 1 Corinthians 13. The home should be the first place that love is demonstrated. Whether you believe it or not, what is demonstrated in the home will stick with the child and it will usually affect the child for good or for bad.

Love-We hear this word daily, for example, when we hear the words, "I love you." This word has been used loosely in our society, however. Many will talk often about love but seldom is that love something that is shown. Love is an action word. God proves this from the beginning of time. He proved that when He gave His only begotten son to die for OUR SINS. When a father goes to labor on a job for 40 hours or more a week to take care of his family, that's love. These days, you will not find many men doing that. There is a call throughout our nation for men to come home.

Will you be that man to answer the call and to return home? I hope so.

Chapter Three

Father Brings Discipline to Children

The American Heritage Dictionary defines discipline as, "training which is expected to produce a special character or pattern of behavior, especially training that produces moral or mental improvement." Self-control is one of those things that discipline brings. It is obtained by enforcing compliance or order. Discipline pays off in the future of the child. We have many institutions in America that are filled with young men and old men who have not been taught discipline in their fatherless homes.

In 1 Samuel 2, Eli was the high priest, and his sons were also priests. Eli rebuked his sons but failed to remove them as priests. They were corrupt, and they played with the women who were assembled at the door of the Tabernacle of Meetings. In 1 Samuel 3:13, the Lord said that He would judge his house for their iniquity which he knew, his sons made themselves vile, and he, Eli, did not restrain them.

This is a case where a father has failed to discipline his sons. If they had been disciplined, they may have seen the error of their ways, but since they were not disciplined, they would continue in their error. Until God said enough is enough. If fathers do not discipline their children, believe me, someone will discipline them. Eli the priest failed to discipline his sons and it would cost his sons their lives. Today, our streets are full of young men who do not have a father to discipline them and now they seem to be out of control. Even behind these prison walls, we see the same behavior. When is it going to stop?

It stops when we get men back in their rightful place, which is the home. The power of parental legacy became clear to me, and it will to you also when you read this prescription from Richard Mather who was a great puritan pastor in the 17th century. He imagined unconverted children on Judgement Day, addressing their parents for neglecting responsibility. "all of this that we have suffered here is through you. You should have taught us things of God and did not. You should have restrained us from sin and corrected us and you did not. You were the means of our final corruption and quietness, and yet you never showed us any competent care, that we may be delivered from it. Woe to you that had no more compassion, and pity to prevent the everlasting misery of your own children."

My friend, I pray that this will not happen to you, or me, as a parent on Judgement Day.

Fathers Bring Guidance to Children

The American Heritage Dictionary defines guidance as, "the act or process of guiding or counseling. One who shows the way by leading, directing, or advising." Your greatest role model should be your fathers and mothers. Their lives should be a life example of a Godly lifestyle. Personally, my mother was my greatest role model. She was an example of a Godly mother. She was the prayer warrior and the spiritual leader in our home.

I like what David said in Psalms 127:3-5. He said, "Behold, children are a heritage from the Lord. The fruit of the womb is a reward. Like arrows in the hand of a warrior. So are the children of one's youth. Happy is the man who has his quiver full of them. They shall not be ashamed. But shall speak with their enemies in the gate."

Too often, children are seen as liabilities rather than assets. The Bible calls children a heritage from the Lord, a reward. We can learn valuable lessons from their inquisitive minds and trusting spirit. Those who view children as a distraction, or a nuisance should instead see them as an opportunity to shape the future. We dare not treat children as an inconvenience when God values them so highly. Children need guidance, just like an arrow in the hand of a warrior. We live in an environment that gives all kinds of guidance and usually it is not governed by the word of God. The advice that is given usually comes from someone's head and not from God's word. Be careful who gives you advice, especially it if is not your parents. Remember, all counsel is not good counsel.

Children's Responsibility to Parents

In Ephesians 6:1-3 it says, "Children, obey your parents in the Lord, for this is right. Honor your father and mother, which is the first commandment with promise, that it may be well with you, and you may live long on the earth." Here we see Paul cites the fifth commandment in Exodus 20:12 and describes it as the first commandment with promise. The promise is to the ones who be obedient to their parents, the one who does this would live long on the earth.

There is a difference between obeying and honoring. To obey means to do as one is told but to honor means to respect and love. God is commanding children to do both. Children are not commanded to disobey God in obeying their parents and children are not asked to be subservient to domineering parents. Children are to obey while under their parent's care, but the responsibility to honor their parents is for life.

Believe it or not, children and parents have a responsibility to each other, and children should honor their parents even if the parents are demanding and unfair. Parents should care in gentle ways for their children, even if the children are disobedient and unpleasant, ideally, of course, Christian parents and Christian children will relate to each other with thoughtfulness and love. This will happen if both parents and children put the other interests above their own—that is, if they submit to one another.

Godly Fathers

Whether you may realize this or not, there is a difference between a father and a Godly father. I have witnessed both and can tell you that the difference is that the physical father fulfills his duties and the Godly father fulfills his physical and spiritual duties. I know that some of you may be asking, "what in the world is he talking about? I thought a father is a father." Well, let me explain myself.

To us, a father is the man who fulfills all of his physical obligations as a father and we do not have to go into all of his duties, believe me, we know them. Now, by the world's standards, for a father, this is a typical father, and we would applaud this guy.

A Godly father is in a relationship with his heavenly father, and he knows that he cannot fulfill his role as a father unless he is in a relationship with his heavenly Father. He seeks guidance from his heavenly father in how to fulfill his God given role as a Godly father. This role is fulfilled in loving his wife as Christ loved the church, in raising his children in the fear and admonition of the Lord and living a Godly life as a believer in his home, on his job, and before his neighbors.

His uttermost desire is to do God's will. Let us pray for more Godly fathers who have the heart of God, and through them we can raise a generation of children who fear God and be obedient to their parents. Godly fathers have been commission by God to pass down the Laws of God to their children and their children's children. In Psalm 78:5-8 it is said, "For he established a testimony in Jacob, and appointed the Law in Israel, which he commanded our fathers. That they should make them known to their children, that the generation to come might know them. The children who would be born. That they may arise and declare them to their children. That they may set their hope in Him." It is important to keep children from repeating the same mistakes as their ancestors.

My friend, what are you doing to pass on the history of God's work to the next generation? Many homes in America have good fathers, but we need more Godly fathers whose hearts have been touched by the master, God, because in the end, which is where it counts, whether or not you are pleasing Him.

Chapter Four

The Need For More Praying Fathers

In Luke 18:1 it states, "Then he spoke a parable to them, that men always ought to pray and not lose heart." Jesus knew the power of prayer and he told his disciples. I never experienced having a praying father around when I was growing up, but I did have the experience of a praying mother. She was a prayer warrior and the spiritual leader of our home. One of my mother's spiritual gifts was the gift of intercession. It is surprising but that is also one of my spiritual gifts also.

The gift of intercession is the special ability that God gives to certain members of the Body of Christ to pray for extended periods of time on a regular basis and see frequent, specific answers to their prayers to a degree much greater than that which is expected of the average Christian. My mother would pray for hours while she was interceding on the behalf of others and their needs.

I cannot remember too many times when I went to her room, and she was not on her knees praying. Back then, they called it talking to God. As a young lad, I was sure that was what she was doing, because no one else was in the room with her so she had to have been talking to God. Today, most of our churches are filled with women who have the spiritual gift of intercession, but there are men who also have this spiritual gift and who pray for hours interceding on the behalf of others and their needs.

I'm reminded back in 2004, for up to about 3 years myself and five other brothers would go into intercession prayer at 12:00 on Saturday and Sunday. For hours, we would all be in one room, on our knees interceding on the behalf of others. When we finished praying, the floor would be wet with tears as we sought the face of God. I cherish those days as I watch grown men who love God intercede for others and their needs. I am reminded of a scripture in Ezekial 22:30 which says, "So I sought for a man among them, who would make a wall, and stand in the gap before me on behalf of the land, that I should not destroy it, but I found no one."

What the people really needed in Ezekial 22:30 was a total spiritual reconstruction and this is what is needed today. Today, God is calling men to stand in the gap for their families. A father is the covering for his family. He is the protector, the supplier, and the spiritual leadership of the home. A father is not at the top of the family but rather, he is at the bottom, he is the foundation of the family. That is how important he is to the family. Today, we need more men to stand up and carry the torch of intercession prayer. I believe that one of the greatest experiences you can witness is a man in love with God.

Coming to Oneself

Did you know that the average man has never discovered himself? That is why we have a society that is filled with abnormal men. In the story of the prodigal son in Luke 15:17, we can see six profound words that lead to the son's transformation, "but when he came to himself." These six profound words can also lead to your transformation if you have not discovered yourself my friend; what will it take to bring you to yourself? Correct thinking, because everything starts with a thought.

The prodigal son had to lose his inheritance in a lifestyle filled with the pleasures of his own lust, and a job feeding swine which was a disgrace in his culture, as well as coming to a place where he was thinking about eating the same slop as the swine ate before he came to himself. My friend, sin will take you where you do not want to go, will keep you longer than you want to stay, and cost you more than you are willing to pay. Did you know that the uttermost penalty for sin is death? This death is a spiritual death, which is eternal separation from God.

Romans 6:23 says, "that the wages of sin is death, but the gift of God is eternal life in Christ Jesus our Lord." The prodigal son came to his wits end. Have you come to your wits end with practicing sin?

In Psalm 107:27-28, it is said, "They reel to and fro and stagger like a drunk man and are at their wits end," but notice, something happens, "then they cried out to the Lord, and He brings them out of the distresses." If you do not have a relationship with Jesus Christ, you are in trouble. If you just happen to die in your sin without Christ, Hell will be your home for all eternity.

Hell is a destiny that involves the free will of a man. God does not condemn you to hell, your choices are what condemns you. I cannot put it any plainer that that. In Luke 13:3 it states, "I tell you nay but unless you repent, you will all likewise perish." The prodigal son cried out from the hog pen. A disgraceful place. You too may be crying out from a place of disgrace. It may be a crack house or a cathouse, or you might be crying out from a penthouse. It may be from a prison cell, or it may be on your deathbed. The place really does not matter, just as long as you are crying out to God.

My friend, He will hear your cry and deliver you out of all of your distresses. Remember when I said earlier that if you do not have Christ, you are in trouble. I made that statement because one day, all of the US will have to stand before God to give an account of all of the deeds we have done in this life. What excuse will you have on judgement day? Romas 1:20 says, "You're left without excuse." My friend, now you have a chance to get right with God. Romans 10:13 says, "For whoever calls on the name of the Lord shall be saved. My friend, you can escape the wrath that is coming to the ungodly if you will call upon the name of the Lord and repent of all of your sins."

When the prodigal son was in an abnormal state, his thinking was not right. Whether you know it or not, your thinking controls your destiny. Thoughts produce actions, actions produce habits, habits produce character, and character produces destiny. Notice everything starts from your thoughts. Now the first thing the prodigal corrected was his thinking, which caused him to look at himself and his condition. Isn't it surprising how incorrect thinking and abnormal behavior will cause you to look at everyone else and their conditions instead of your own?

Correct thinking will cause you to look at yourself before you look at others. My friend, I don't care how bad you have messed up, you can return home. Your father, God, is waiting with arms outstretched for you to return home. The prodigal son got up from where he was because the lifestyle, he was living was beneath him. Any lifestyle that practices ungodliness is a lifestyle that is beneath you. God created you to bring Him glory in everything that you do. God gets no glory out of a lifestyle of sin and ungodliness.

You were created for much more. He has a better life for you. John 10:10 states, "He wants you too have life and have it more abundantly." Jesus died to set you free from the yoke of sin and death. As I close, if you want to know what's normal or abnormal thinking and behavior then turn to your Bible. It is the word of God and the mind of God. He alone sets the standards for what is normal or abnormal thinking and behavior, no one and nothing else sets those standards but God.

The prodigal son was caught up in abnormal behavior all because he had abnormal thinking. When he came to himself, a transformation took place in his life. He also had a loving father waiting every day for his return home. I do not know whom I am talking to through this message, but there is somebody out there who needs to return home physically or spiritually. If it is physically, I hope you have read the statistics of this epidemic of fatherless homes and where your children stand in your absence. I pray that these statistics move you to take actions in returning home.

If it is spiritually, I want you to know that transformation is waiting on you when you come to yourself and your correct thinking. Here is a prayer that I want you to say and mean it from the depths of your heart and watch God work in your life.

Father God,
Forgive me for going astray.
I was caught up in the lust of my flesh.
I've failed you and my family.
Please forgive me of all my sins.
I acknowledge that I have done wrong
and I repent of all the wrong I've done.
I accept Christ as my Lord and Savior.
Right now, I submit my life to you and your will,
and Father please help me to be reconciled with my family.
I ask this in Jesus' name, your son, Amen.

Chapter Five

The Scars of Yesterday

Did you know that Mephibosheth is one of the few characters in the Bible who was never healed. He became lame through an unfortunate accident which was no fault of his own. He was just five years old when his nurse found out that his father Jonathan and his grandfather Saul had been killed in battle in 1 Samuel 31:1-6. Now, in 2 Samuel 4:1-4, we see that the nurse took him up and she fled. As she was fleeing however, she accidentally dropped Mephibosheth. He became lame in both of his legs from being dropped.

I wonder how many children today have been dropped by their fathers either accidentally or on purpose. The scars from that moment would forever change this five-year-old lad's life. Can you imagine what he was thinking at that moment? Yesterday he was running around and playing with his friends as kids do but the next day, he is lame in both of his legs while looking out his window while watching the other kids play without him. He was also dealing with the death of his father and his grandfather on top of being lame for the rest of his life.

They say that when it rains, it pours. It certainly was true in Mephibosheth's life. Now what will become of this five-year-old boys' self-esteem? In other words, how will he see himself from then on? Truly, it would affect him because in 2 Samuel 9:8, we read that he considered himself as a dead dog. He had low self-esteem. How would his friends see him from now on; you know children can be very cruel at times, especially to the handicap. What would become of his dreams? You know at this age every child has dreams of becoming someone great. Would he become bitter with his life? Would he need counseling? Who would take care of him now since his father and grandfather had been killed?

These are some tough questions. Now I want to know, how many of you still carry the scars from yesterday? We all do. In Romans 3:23 it says, "That all have sinned and fall short of the glory of God." We are all born with scars from yesterday. The stain of sin was passed down through our fallen forefather, Adam. Romans 5:19 states this clearly.

There are some of you who still carry scars from a bitter divorce. There are some of you who still carry scars from alcohol or drug addiction. There are some of you who still carry scars from a bad tattoo and now you wish you had never gotten it. There are some of you who still carry scars from being incarcerated and you tell yourself daily, "How could I have been so stupid?" There are some of you who still carry scars from being fired from the first job. Believe it or not, but that may have been what pushed you to start selling drugs or committing crimes to get money.

There are some of you who carry scars from being abandoned by a mother or father. There are some of you who carry scars from the death of a loved one be it mother, father, sister, brother, or maybe a childhood friend. There are some of you who carry scars from your first sweetheart breakup, and that is why you have a hard time committing to a relationship because you find it hard to trust someone and this is because of those scars that still remain. There are some of you who carry scars from being sexually abused by an adult when you were just a child.

There are some of you who carry scars from lost opportunities that have made you become bitter. My friend, if one of these is you, I want you to know that you are not alone, believe me. Any problem that you face—and even the worst of the worst of problems, have already been encountered by someone in the Bible. The scriptures graphically record the struggle and the victory of those who place their trust in God. That gives us hope. If God is truly not a respecter of person as Romans 2:11 says, then he will do for us the same things that he has done for others.

We can live vicariously through the lives of the Bible characters and hope for the situations that we encounter. The main scars I am speaking about are memories of bad decisions, bad incidents, or choices that we have made one time or another in our lives. Many of you have made bad decisions when you were younger, and now you have learned from your mistakes. There are some of you who are young who think that you have forever to change, but the Bible says that tomorrow is not a promise.

Did you know that scars and memories can be good if they are used to draw strength from? Then again, scars and memories can be harmful if you allow them to dictate your life and future. Remember what I said earlier: failure is an event, not a person. Well, I have news for you. You are not a failure; you have only had a setback and you are getting ready to make a comeback.

The word dictate means to rule or control. Never let your past failures rule or control your future. We have all made bad choices and certainly had some bad experience one time or another. The Apostle Paul had been Saul before his conversion, and he had done some bad things to God's people. Even after his conversion, I am pretty sure that his memories reminded him of his past life. There were scars that he had to carry with him to his grave, but he knew that God had forgiven him, and he did not live in condemnation after his conversion. Neither should you, my friend.

If you have confessed and repented of your sins, you are forgiven. I do not care how many times the devil tries to bring it up because you are forgiven of ALL of your sins. I like what Apostle Paul wrote in Philippians 3:13-14, "I do not count myself to have apprehended, but one thing, I do, forgetting those things which are behind, reaching forward to those things which are ahead. I press toward the goal for the prize of the upward call of God in Christ Jesus." The main thing that Paul is letting us know is that he did not let his past dictate and rule his future and that you should not either.

Remember the scars that Jesus bore at Calvary. Those scars did not stop him from getting out of the grave on resurrection Sunday. My friend, you must not let the scars of yesterday stop you from being the man God wants you to be. Physically, Calvary was a horrible sight but spiritually, it was God's will. Just read Isaiah 53:10, "Please the Lord to bruise him. He hath put him to grief, when you make his soul an offering for sin. He shall see his seed. He shall prolong his days. And the pleasure of the Lord shall prosper in his hand."

My friend, God wants to turn your scars into stars, and your mess into a message. Have you ever wondered how you survived through all that you have been through? It was God. He has been working things out for you from the day you were born. He has a plan and a purpose for your life. Just look what he says about you in Jeremiah 29:11, "For I know the thoughts that I think towards you, says the Lord, thoughts of peace and not of evil, to give you a future and a hope."

Believe it or not, but some of you should have been dead a long time ago. Some of you should have caught AIDS. Some of you should have gotten more time in prison. The reason why none of these things happened is all because of His Grace.

Romans 2:4 says, "The goodness of God leads to repentance," not the wrath of God, which is what religion teaches. God showed you mercy when you did not deserve it and that is why we call it Grace, which is an unmerited favor. If not for God's grace, an unmerited favor, I would have been dead a long time ago. My friend, you too would have been dead a long time ago if it was not for the Grace of God, an unmerited favor.

Now Mephibosheth had a bad perception of himself for years. David took him to his palace and restored him to the estate of Saul. David appointed servants to him, and then gave him a place at the royal table. 2 Samuel 9:7-13 states, "Yesterday, he was in Lo-Debar, a pasture-less place. Now he is sitting at the kings table, a place of plenty." My friend, God has a seat for you at His table. I know you still carry scars from yesterday, but remember, you are forgiven, and you have been invited to come and sit, rest, and eat.

Chapter Six

Testimony Of My Father's Last Days

I stated before that the spiritual leadership in our home was my mother, Martha Baker. That is not taking anything from my Dad as being the head of the household. However, it was my mother who had a relationship with God and my dad did not during those days. My mother was more concerned about God's will and His purpose for her families lives than my dad was in those days.

My mother passed away from cancer in 1984. At that time, I felt that the world had come to an end, at least my world. The Lord comforted my sister, brothers, and I during those dark hours of our lives. At that time, my dad and I became close after my mother's death. I believe it bothered him that he had not been as close to his children as he should have been and now, he had been given an opportunity to make amends.

What better time to do it than then, so he took advantage of the opportunity that he had to reach out to his children. There were four of us, including myself and my sister Vondell, as well as my brothers Anthony and Stanley. My mother had requested that I raise my younger two brothers. Some how she saw a leadership role in me who was twenty-four years old at the time.

My dad knew it was better for us to stay together, so he had no problem with me raising my two brothers. At this time, he had another home and another family. We agreed to let my younger brothers stay with him on the weekends and in the summer when school was out. He became a great part of their lives. He attended my younger brothers football games and would take them on vacations with him. My sister and I would go to his home often to visit with him. I had wished my mother could witness our relationship.

I got married a year after my mother's death and my wife and I raised my two brothers as our own son's. A few years later, I heard that my father had cancer through my sister Vondell. He had not wanted me to know. I guess he did not want me to worry about him. I had just lost my mother to cancer and now my father had it, and they said it was terminal. They say when it rains, it pours…I certainly felt wet.

At that time, my grandmother took my father in to stay with her so that she could attend to him in his last days. At the time, hospice also went to my grandmother's home to attend to my fathers needs. Hospice is a program that provides palliative care and attends to the emotion and spiritual needs of the terminally ill patients in an inpatient facility or at the patients' home.

My grandmothers heart hoped that my dad would be saved before he left this world. She anointed him with oil and prayed over him. She read him scriptures from the Bible daily. I remember one day visiting him at my grandmother's home, he said to me that all he wanted was for his soul to be saved. Those words still ring in my ears today. Believe it or not, God had him in the right place, at the right time, with the right people.

My grandmother was a true woman of God, and the God in her was not going to stand by and watch her son go to Hell. A mother's Love. I called my grandmother and the Hospice workers God's Angels. Hebrews 23:2 states, "Do not forget to entertain strangers, for so doing some have unwittingly entertained angels."

I remember the last visit to my grandmother's home while my father was still alive. I could see in his eyes that he would soon be gone to eternity. I sensed this in my spirit at the time and sure enough, a few days later they called me at my job and told me that my dad had passed away. I left my job and went straight to my grandmother's home.

All the other family members were already there at that time. When I walked into the door of my grandmother's home, she came and hugged me and these are the words that she spoke, "Warren, he made it in." After hearing those words, a peace came over me. Right then I knew that it was well with my father's soul. I felt it in my spirit that my father had made peace with God. God had given him another chance to get right with his children. The Bible calls that Grace—unmerited favor.

It all came back to me at the moment, that I would hear my mother telling my father that God was going to save him. In those days, he would make comments that she did not know what she was talking about, but she did. She was standing on the word of God. She did not know when, but she knew by her faith that God was going to save my dad.

She stood on 1 Corinthians 7:14, "For the unbelieving husband is sanctified by the wife, and the unbelieving wife is sanctified by the husband, otherwise your children would be unclean, but now they are holy." Apostle Paul is not saying that just because one parent is saved that the whole family is saved. He is saying that now your family has some Godly influence in the home and now the prayers of that righteous person in the home can intercede on behalf of the rest of the family.

Now they have a better chance of being saved than they had before there was no righteous person in the house. Now, through the lifestyle of that righteous parent, there is an example of Christ in the home, and the rest of the people in the home can be won for Christ. My mother lived a holy life before my dad and her children. Daily he saw Christ in her life. She was the spiritual leadership in our home. She was the prayer warrior of the family and she prayed regularly that God would save her household.

She went to her grave believing that God was going to save my Dad, and God did save my dad. Today, my father and mother are in the presence of God. My friend, you may have a loved one who does not know Christ as their Lord and savior. Keep on praying and believing God's word. I have seen prayer work in many situations in my life and in the lives of others.

Chapter Seven

Becoming a Man

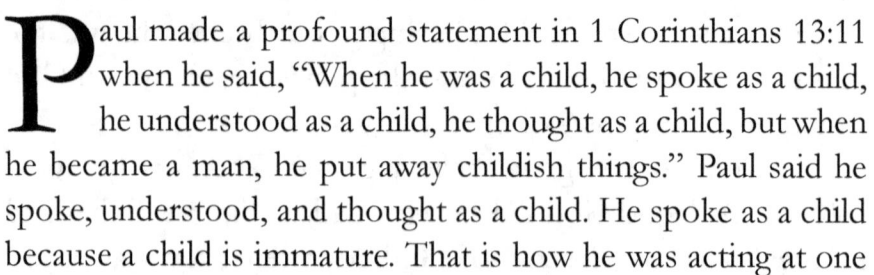

Paul made a profound statement in 1 Corinthians 13:11 when he said, "When he was a child, he spoke as a child, he understood as a child, he thought as a child, but when he became a man, he put away childish things." Paul said he spoke, understood, and thought as a child. He spoke as a child because a child is immature. That is how he was acting at one time in his life, even though, physically, he was a grown man.

He went on to say, "BUT." Don't you like when the word BUT comes into play? You just know something is going to happen, BUT I became a man. I put away immature behavior. He acknowledges that his speech, understanding, and his thoughts had been immature. As he matured, there had been a process that had taken place, because he used the word, "became," and it is in the past tense of become, as he walked into his manhood. True manhood is spiritual, emotional, and physical. When he stated that he put away, he means that he laid it aside.

Bad behavior or thoughts and speech and a lack of understanding has to be put away before you can walk into your full manhood. Have you seen a man who is full grown physically and yet is speaking foolishly? Or a physically full-grown man who has no comprehension? Usually, most of our problems come from our thinking being wrong. Your actions are a by-product of your thoughts. If you think wrong, you will do wrong. Your actions follow your thoughts. Proverbs 23:7 says, "As a man thinks in his heart so is he." Now if you want to become a man, spiritually, physically and emotionally, you can, but you have to envision one.

You cannot become what you can not envision because you become what you envision. If you envision yourself as a pimp, drug dealer, player or in prison you will find yourself walking in that path. To become a real man, you must know and envision a real man. Here is the best example of a real man. Paul came to know him personally in 1 Corinthians 11:1, "Imitate me, just as I imitate Christ."

Now, I know that you may be wondering why Paul said to imitate him as he imitates Christ. Why could he not say, "Imitate Christ, as I imitate Christ?" Well, there is a reason that Paul says, "imitate me," first. He was not being arrogant, nor did he consider himself to be sinless. At this time, however, the Corinthian believers did not know much about the life and ministry of Christ. Paul could not tell them to imitate Jesus, because the Gospels had not yet been written, so they did not know what Jesus was like.

The best way to point these new Christians to Christ was to point them to a Christian in whom they trusted. Paul had been in Corinth for two years and had built a relationship of trust with many of these new believers. That is why he said, "imitate me, as I imitate Christ." Jesus Christ is our perfect example of a complete man, physically, spiritually, and emotionally. Paul had to envision what he wanted to become, so he envisioned Christ and then he patterned his life after Christ.

Our young men need mentors like Paul who will help and teach them to be men like Christ. What better example of a man than Christ? Personally, I have had a lot of mentors in my life, and they were truly men and women of God who imitated Christ daily in their walk with God. I think of them often.

Today, it seems like the drug dealers, the pimps, the players and the convicts have become our young boys role models. I could see if they had changed their lives, but to idolize these guys and worship the ground that they walk upon is crazy. It let me know that something is wrong. America, we have to get serious about the future generations of our young men and young women. Can we afford to let another generation go this way? We sit still and say nothing. We do nothing to educate our young boys and girls on the importance of them being a positive role model. No wonder the gangs are taking over our streets, because we have become silent, or should I say, we have become just plain scared, which is a condition or sensation of sudden fear.

Believe it or not, this is what many of our citizens have become today, plain scared and traumatized by the violence in our streets. It's time to take back our young men from the pimps, the gangs, drug dealers, and the players clubs and teach them how to be a real men. We must also remember that manhood is a process. Boys do not become men overnight. We have to be patient with them so that they can fully develop in to mature men.

If you do not raise them, someone else will and you may not like what they become. Today, many of our young men are living a life of fantasy. Believe me when I say that this life, they are living is fantasy, fictional. They need mentors who will teach them the real facts of life, not this fictional stuff. Remember when I said, "What you envision, you become." Well, we need to display—which means to present or hold up to view, positive images of Godly men doing the right things.

Isn't it surprising how the bad news gets more attention than the good news? We spend more time and money promoting all the bad that goes on in our nation than the good that goes on in our nation. Have we become consumed with negativity so much that we promote it to that level? At times, I watch the world news and it's about 30 minutes. They spend twenty-five minutes talking about all the bad news, what usually happens throughout the day or night, and the last five minutes they will show someone doing something good or positive. For twenty-five minutes however, commercials included, they give you all the bad news that happens.

When you do see a positive story, your spirit is grieved from that last twenty-five minutes of bad news that you have seen. I see why our young men want to be gangbangers. It is because they publicize the drug dealers, gangs, pimps and the players lifestyle right before their eyes every single day, and on most channels all day. That is not even mentioning Hollywood, or should I say Helliwood. They portray drugs, sex, gangs, violence, and any immoral lifestyle they can come up with in their movies. If we are going to teach our young boys how to become men, then we must be the men that we want them to be. They need Godly examples, because if not, then they will envision what is on display before them, and believe me, the world has a lot to offer them…and it is not Godly.

A Testimony of a Young Man Who Lived in a Dysfunctional Home

I was born September 5th, 1993, in Atlanta, Georgia. I was raised on the westside on Hollywood Road. I am 22 years old. My name is Gregory Grier, and I grew up with my sister and my brother. My mom sold drugs and worked two jobs and my dad was a full-time robber and drug dealer. He beat my mom, but his lifestyle caught up with him when I was about 4 years old. He had been shot five times and he almost died, but through the grace of God he survived though he was left paralyzed.

Now, when it came to me, he figured that money was everything. Instead of spending time with the family, he figured spending money was more important. I am my mom's youngest child, and my dads only child. I was a confused child. They fought over me a lot about things concerning my wellbeing. They separated after he got shot, because he could not control her mentally and physically, so that was her chance to get away.

We were living in the hood on a low income, but it had its advantages. It could be fun and miserable all at the same time. It was fun because as a kid, I got the chance to play with a lot of children in the neighborhood. It was also miserable because I was a child but still had to think as an adult because my mom was selling drugs and working so much that my siblings and I had to make our decisions on our own. My grandmother would watch us, but she also did drugs.

My mom tried so many relationships after our father left, but being in the hood, all of them were gangsters and drug dealers. It did not feel good seeing other kids spending time with their dads when mine would not even pick up the phone because he did not want to deal with my mom. I remember three times when my mom's boyfriend would fight her. I had seen that in the past with my dad and I refused to let anybody do that to her again.

At a young age, I had fought a lot of men about my mom. I always thought, "How can they protect her when all they want to do is fight her?" I have always been overprotective of my mom. My dad never came to anything dealing with me, school, or just life period. I still respect him as my father, however. My mom never kept me away from him, but he did not want me as a responsibility.

When I was 12 years old, my mom forced me to move in with him, because of the trouble that I was getting into. I was a strain on my mom because I was always fighting while I was growing up or I was disorderly to my teachers at school. She would keep leaving her job to come get me from school. She grew tired of that after so many years and she decided that it was my dad's turn. My dad agreed and my mom then enrolled me into Brown Middle School off cascade, behind the Kroger plaza.

Dad never allowed me to live with him permanently because he was so used to taking care of himself that he did not know me as a person besides his son. So, I, as a person, was new to him. I was already half the age that I am now. He could not handle the person that I had become or the destructive child that I had grown up to be without any proper guidance. After

6 months of living with him, he packed all of my stuff up early one morning and dropped me off at my mom's doorstep.

He pulled off before she even knew that I was outside. When he would do stuff like that or make promises then lie, I always cried. Never boo-hoo cries, but tears would roll down my face. I would hide from people or just would not talk for hours. People would say that I had an attitude problem. They did not know me as a person or how the things my dad did were making me feel. I had been misunderstood my whole life. I cannot blame my dad for my actions, I can only blame him for my emotions as a child.

I struggled for 18 years every day by my mom's side. My brother and sister left at ages 15 and 16 but I stayed everyday with my mom, mostly because I was scared some thug would try and hurt her. I was used to drama, and I did not want her to go through that by herself. People never understood why I was such a momma's boy and that is because they did not understand that I never had a male figure to take the worries of someone hurting my mom off of my shoulders.

To this day, my mom is the only one who has been there for me, for better or for worst. Now that I am grown as a man myself, I use my bad experiences from not having a father to better myself to raise my two daughters and love them the way my mom showed me how to. A father can make a big difference in the world if he takes time out from his busy schedule and gives that time to the child who needs it physically, mentally and spiritually.

Now, I am a father with two daughters. I have always wanted a son, but God put two females in my life for a reason. I am currently in prison with 20 due 5 but the Lord has used prison to open my eyes and to look at life experiences with a different perspective. I have made decisions that have caused my daughters mother and I to separate. I have not talked to them verbally in four months.

That time made me realize how much I love her. It made me realize that my kids need me and her to agree and disagree for the mental and emotion health of my girls. I finally called her on the phone, and she told me how much she and my girls love me. That lightened the burden that I have been carrying for a while because my mind and heart was focused on being there for my family.

A child needs the security of their father. It is a dominant love that child feels that makes the child feel safe. My point is that a father's role is very important to a child's life. Now, it is my time to turn my experiences with my father into something positive and become a bigger man for my baby girls because they need me, and I need them.

Chapter Eight

More Statistics on the Absence of Fathers in the Home

I quoted three statistics at the beginning of the book. This was just to let you know what the statistics say about the absence of fathers in the home. I do not know if you have taken those numbers lightly or not, but I am compelled in my spirit to quote you a few more at this time, so you will not take for granted the importance of fathers in their children's lives. Here are some more statistics.

63% of youth who commit suicide come from fatherless homes, (Department of health and human services, Bureau of Census). 90% of all homeless and runaway children are from fatherless homes. 85% of all children that exhibit behavioral disorders come from fatherless homes, (CDC). 85% of rapists motivated with displaced anger come from fatherless homes,

(Criminal Justice-Behavior, 1978). 75% of all adolescent patients in chemical abuse centers come from fatherless homes, (Rainbow For All God's Children).

I have quoted these statistics to you but believe me when I say that there are more. I have just quoted enough to get your attention on the fact that we have a serious problem with the absence of fathers in the home. I pray that someone will notice and do something about it because we cannot continue to lose our children to this epidemic we call, "fatherless homes."

Becoming Mentors to our Young Men and Women Behind Prison Walls

Adopt a Prison Project

The Adopt A Prisoner project is a ministry based upon the principals of giving oneself as a mentor to an individual who is incarcerated behind prison walls, either males or females. This ministry offers any church organization or individual the opportunity to be a blessing through the act of mentorship. It involves those who are less fortunate; the ones whom society has called, "the scum of the earth," whether socially, spiritually, or financially.

The fact that this ministry has been established to help those who are incarcerated does not lessen the urgency to take part in it. If anything, this presents an even more visible reason to participate. The foundational scripture from the APP ministry is based on Matthew 25:31-46 which says, "When the son of man comes in his glory, and he will separate them one from another, as a shepherd divides his sheep from the goats. And he set the sheep on his right hand, but the goats on the left. Then the king will say to those on his right hand, 'come, you blessed of my father, inherit the Kingdom prepared for you from the foundation of the world; for I was hungry and you gave me food; I was thirsty and you gave me drink; I was a stranger and you took me in; I was naked and you clothed; I was sick and you visited me; I was in prison and you came to me. Then the righteous will answer him saying, 'Lord, when did we see you hungry and feed you, or thirsty and give you drink? When did we see you as a stranger and take you in or naked and clothe you? When did we see you sick, or in prison, and come to you?' And the king will answer and say to them, 'Assuredly, I say to you, inasmuch as you did it to one of the least of these my brethren, you did it to me.' Then he will also say to those on the left hand, 'Depart from me, you cursed, into the everlasting punishment.'"

In this portion of scripture, Jesus teaches his disciples a most revealing and inspiring lesson. The setting of this lesson is the day of judgement that comes with the return of Jesus Christ. Of course, the judgement, separation, and everlasting punishment by fire is imposed upon those that failed to attend to the needs of their neighbor when they knew him to be hungry, thirsty, homeless, naked, sick, and in prison.

In contrast to this terrible judgement, Jesus expounds on the blessing and eternal inheritance promised to those who did attend to their neighbor when they recognized him to be in such dire circumstances. The common question asked by both the righteous and the cursed; "when did we understand you to be in our situation?" The answer that the Lord gives is a timeless affinity to the necessity of compassion and brotherly love.

Just as you have chosen or refused to attend to the needs of the least of your brother, so have you done the same to the Lord of glory. The word of God states that we are all under sin. Read Romans 3:19-24 and Galatians 3:22…that none is better than another. Romans 2:11 says, "And that God is not a respecter of person." 2 Corinthians 5:10 further guarantees that we shall all appear before the judgement seat of Christ.

Romans 14:10 states that it is in vain to judge one another for naught. One of the most sobering facts to consider, which is that the judgement must begin at the house of God. 1 Peter 4:17-18 affirms that even the righteous will scarcely be saved. Let us also be aware that sin is not merely restricted to the act of doing evil, but also in refusing to perform that which is good.

James 4:17 tells us that the focus of ministry is not a kingdom call to repentance, but a wake-up call to action. This scripture passage illustrates the absolute necessity of our works in addition to our profession of faith toward a brother or sister who is naked and destitute. This example is in no way intended to establish our faith through works, but rather, declares that good works are an unconditional result of the very faith which we profess.

Any other faith without action is vain, empty and lifeless. Again, we remind you that the heart and mission of our ministry is not only to bless others. It is also to allow you the opportunity to be a blessing beyond measure to other, (Luke 6:38). It would be remiss of us to stress that giving does not always demand financial support. Often times letters, cards and words of encouragement have a worth far above that of any monetary value. Do you know that one word from God can change a person's life? If God has given you that word of eternal life for someone behind these prison walls, I encourage you to share it with someone.

Proverbs 18:21 says, "Death and life are in the power of the tongue." Did you know, that as a Christian, you have power to impart life to a young man or woman? Yes, they have strayed away but who has not? Paul states in 1 Corinthians 6:11, "that such were some of you." Romans 6:23 states, "all have sinned and fall short of the glory of God." Be assured that through your mentorship, men and women can change their lives.

Yes, they too can become a productive member of society again. I encourage you to sow the seed of being a mentor today and remember that it can start with a letter. Believe me, someone is waiting to hear from you. I also encourage you who are older and behind prison walls to become a positive influence on the young men who just started their sentence. God has given you another opportunity to help someone in the right way.

To begin this mentorship, you will need to go to the Georgia Department of Corrections website at www.dcor.state.ga.us. It is public information. You can find names, addresses, and GDC numbers of male and female inmates who are incarcerated. If you are in another state, you can go to your states Corrections Department and find some young man or woman to correspond with.

I strongly recommend that male mentors select male mentees and female mentors select female mentees to avoid any pitfalls from the enemy. I encourage you to pray and let the Holy Spirit led you to whom you should correspond with. If the APP is not for you, please pass the information on to someone else. I would never advise you to do anything that is not God's will for your life, but I could advise you to pray for the others who have chosen to become mentors. As I come to the end of this appeal, my prayers for you are centered in the promises of God's word. In blessing others, you will be blessed.

Chapter Nine

When Children become Mothers and Fathers

I remember when I was growing up, I would watch kids in the neighborhood play a game that they would call, "playhouse". In this game, the children would dress up as adults and some would be parents, and some would play the kids. It was just what it was called, playhouse. Well, today, children do not play, "playhouse." They are actually living, "playhouse," because it is their reality.

Today, children are becoming mothers and fathers without knowing that parenting is not a game that you play in your back yard. Parenting is real, believe me. There is a difference in playing the role and actually being the parents. Parenting is a 24/7 job with no days off. Just because a young boy can make a baby does not mean he is ready financially, emotionally, physically, and spiritually to be a father. We have seen many boys make babies while not matured enough to handle the responsibilities of being a father. Just because a young girl can get pregnant and have a baby does not mean she is ready to become a mother. There is a lot that goes in to parenting than just the title of mother and father.

A few years ago, I read a statistic that stated that 55% of our youth in High school have had sex by the time they graduated. When I read that report, I said to myself, "What are they learning in school?" It is certainly not what we as parents planned. We call them Baby Boomers because it is the time when births of babies are booming. Believe it or not, that is what we have today; a baby booming society.

Children are having children. As parents, we need to teach our children the importance of saving themselves for marriage. I know our modern society believes that we should aid them in protection, because "kids will be kids." Personally, I believe that when you hand them condoms and birth control pills, it is just like you are giving them permission to do as they please. Many parents believe that they are going to do it anyway, so why not educate them on the importance of protecting themselves with the use of condoms and birth control pills to prevent unwanted children?

I am never against education, but I do stand for abstinence because the Bible teaches it. Safe sex is no sex until marriage and I cannot put it any plainer than that. I know you may be saying that this is old school, and that the world does not live in those days anymore. Well, it may be old school to tell and teach your young girls and boys to save themselves for marriage, but it is right, and it is in the Bible.

1 Corinthians 7:1-2 says, "Now concerning the things of which you wrote to me. It is good for a man not to touch a woman, nevertheless, because of sexual immorality, let each man have his own wife, and let each woman have her own husband." I know that many of you believe that the Bible is old fashioned and that we need to change with the times, but these thoughts are what has gotten us in trouble before. Everyone doing what they call right and just going with the times.

My friend, the Bible is our counselor. It is very important that we search the scriptures before we make decisions to go with the times. As a matter of fact, do you really know what times you are talking about going with? The Bible says in 2 Timothy 3:1-5 that we are living in perilous times. That verse goes on to list the conditions of men's hearts during these times. Now, I do not think that you want to be a part of this crowd, because in verse 5, the last portion of the scripture it states, "and from such people, turn away."

My friend, I encourage you to follow God's word, because if you go by it, you will save yourself a lot of headaches, money, time and consequences of bad decisions. When a 13- or 15-year-old girl gets pregnant, what happens to her childhood? It means that she will have to grow up quickly and prepare herself to be mother when she is still only a child herself.

The next question, what happens to school? Usually, they quit. Now, where is the father? Good question. Most of the time, he got what he wanted, and he is gone because he is too immature to take responsibility for his actions. Sometimes, you will find a few who will rise to the occasion and take the responsibility of raising his son or daughter but in the meantime, there will be life's challenges because they are children who are raising children.

It's time for us as parents to share with our children our bad choices that we have made and the consequences we have had to endure from making those bad choices. We should also share with our children the importance of saving themselves for marriage. Believe it or not, I am hearing about a lot of adults who are saving themselves for marriage the second go around and they find themselves doing this God's way this time, which will save them a lot of misery.

If you can get your children to listen to bad decisions that you made at their age, maybe they will not repeat your bad mistakes. Just maybe, it will open their eyes to how important it is to save themselves until marriage. This goes for boys and girls. When a boy gets a girl pregnant and she has a baby for him, he too has many challenges for which he is not prepared. He too will have to be a father before his time. Whether he can handle the responsibility of taking care of his newfound family or not, only God knows.

It's time that we as parents build a relationship with our children so that when we do instruct them in a matter, they will feel and know that we are doing it out of our love for them and that they to do not make the same wrong decisions that we made in our youth. Children seldom listen to someone that they do not trust.

We as parents must build trust with our children for them to listen to us, and maybe we can put a dent in children becoming fathers and mothers.

Hypocritical Parents

In Matthew 23:1-3, we see Jesus speaking to the multitudes and also his disciples. He says, "The scribes and Pharisees sit in Moses's seat. Therefore, whatever they tell you to observe, that observe and do, but do not do according to their works: for they say, and do not do." Now in verse 13, Jesus calls them hypocrites. The Pharisees traditions and their interpretations and applications of the law had become as important to them as God's law itself.

Their laws were not all bad—some were beneficial. The problem arose when the religious leaders, 1. Took man made rules as seriously as God's laws, 2. Told the people to obey these rules, but did not do so themselves, 3. Obeyed rules not to honor God but to make themselves look good. Jesus did not condemn what the Pharisees taught but what they were, hypocrites.

Jesus again exposed the hypocritical attitudes of the religious leaders. They knew the scriptures but did not live by them. They did not care about being holy—they cared about looking holy in order to receive the people's admiration and praise. Today, like the Pharisees, many people who know the Bible do not let it change their lives. They say that they follow Jesus, but they do not live by his standards of love. People who live this way are hypocrites. We must make sure that our actions match our words.

If the truth were told, we have all played the hypocrite role in one way or another. Even today, many are still playing that role. Whether you are a saint or a sinner, you have played that part. Many of us parents know that we have played that part, because we have asked our children to not do this or that and we have been guilty of it ourselves…hypocrites. Many parents are still playing the hypocrite role because we want be transparent with our children, whether you know it or not, hypocrisy is a lie. It is practicing and professing a belief, feeling or virtues that one does not hold or possess. It is falseness.

We set rules for our children and we ourselves break our own rules. What do we expect our children to do when they see us do the opposite of what we told them not to do? A lot of parents tell their children, "Do what I say, not as I do," or, "I'm the parent, you are supposed to listen to me," or, "I'm grown," like that is supposed to excuse them from not being truthful. Still, they are playing the role of the hypocrite not knowing that children usually do what they see their parents do.

Most often you will find children imitating their parents, especially the little ones. I remember growing up in our neighborhood when I would hear other children using profanity. One day, I asked one of those kids where he had learned to curse like that, and he said he had learned it from his mother. I asked him did his mother allow him to curse and he said that she curses, he had figured that he was allowed too as well.

Let us just confirm what the Bible says about this. In 1 Corinthians 15:33 it is said, "Do not be deceived; evil company corrupts good habits." Well, the company that this young boy was keeping was his mother. He lived in the house with her and that bad profanity that he learned came right out of her mouth. There is a chance that she did not realize that he would pick it up, but he did pick it up, nevertheless. It did not sound good coming out of the mouth of a child.

Children are sponges and they soak up whatever it is that they hear. Be careful what you are saying when you are around them because it is not funny when you hear it coming out of their mouths for the second go around. We as parents should be lights to our children in a positive way and we must practice what we preach. Too often we will tell our children all the dos and don'ts when we do not practice those things ourselves and when we do this, we are playing the role of a hypocrite.

If parents are not going to set standards in the home, then who will? We certainly cannot let the children set the standards, or our homes would be in chaos. Parents, it is time out for playing the hypocrite role, living lies, hiding behind masks, and as some would say, "faking the funk," because in the end times, it is going to catch up with you and the true you will be exposed.

You might fool some people some of the time, but you cannot fool God none of the time. That is why it is very important that you be transparent with your children, because when you tell them not to drink alcohol and then they see you coming home drunk as a skunk, you have just become a hypocrite to them because that is how you have portrayed yourself to them.

Most of the time, our children know us better than we know them. If you do have an addiction, be transparent with them and get help and let them see the change you have made. Honesty is the best way. If you lie to them and preach what you do not practice yourself, then when they do find that you did not practice what you preach, you will lose their trust. This is one of the worst things a parent can lose with their children, their trust. The other is their love, and these two things usually go hand in hand with each other. When a child trusts his parents, he or she will come to them with anything. When a child is betrayed, it takes time for that parent to gain that child's trust again. As parents, we cannot afford to go on like it is business as usual, playing the role of the hypocrite. It's time that we practice what we preach.

Chapter Ten

Learning to Forgive

Children Forgiving Absent Fathers

I know that you have heard it said before that when you harbor unforgiveness in your heart, it is similar to injecting poison into one's veins. It affects you, not the other person. Now, most people think that if I forgive him or her, I am letting them off of the hook. Forgiveness does not exonerate or acquit the other person who hurt you, nor does it trivialize or lessen the depth of your trauma.

Now what it does do is liberate you and free you and your soul from living in bitterness and strife for the rest of your life. In Matthew 6:14-15, Jesus says, "If you forgive men their trespasses, your heavenly father will also forgive you. But if you do not forgive men their trespasses, neither will your father forgive your trespasses." We see here where Jesus gives a startling warning about forgiveness: if we refuse to forgive others, God will also refuse to forgive us. Why? Because when we do not forgive others, we are denying our common ground as sinners in need of God's forgiveness.

God's forgiveness of sin is not the direct result of our forgiving others, but it is based on our realizing what forgiveness means. Read Ephesians 4:32. For some of us, it is easy for us to ask God for forgiveness, but difficult to grant it to others. Whenever we ask God to forgive us for our sins, we should ask ourselves, "Have I forgiven the people who wronged me?" Forgiveness is about letting things go, writing it off. I know that it may be hard, but for your survival, you have got to let it go. In the long run, holding onto it will only hurt you.

I shared a letter from you that I received from my son Desmond when he graduated from high school. Well, I also got a visit from him in 2008. He shared with me that he had forgiven me. He said, "Dad, I forgive you." When he said those words, my eyes got water. I knew in my heart that it was the working of God in his life. Then he said, "I never want us to talk about the past, neither will I ever ask you to explain yourself to me. I forgive you." He knew that he could not live his life harboring unforgiveness in his heart towards me or anyone else.

Now, him forgiving me did not exonerate me or acquit me from the hurt that I have caused him. It liberated him from living the rest of his life in bitterness and anger towards me, however. Most people who hurt us are not really thinking about our needs when they hurt us at all and neither did, we when we hurt them. They were just thinking of themselves—self-centeredness.

The father who abandoned his children did not think about his children's needs. He only thought of himself. The drug addicted parents did not think about their children, but only thought of the next high. The husband who cheated on his wife only thought of himself and his lust.

James 1:14 says, "But each one is temped when he is drawn away by his own desires and enticed." Afterwards, he lives in regrets, and they live in bitterness and anger for not being there for them. If we want to walk in forgiveness, we must be prepared to talk about our problems. You will never conquer what you will not confront. Remember that forgiveness is not a memory lapse, but a rather, a memory release.

If someone askes for your forgiveness, give it. Release them from their self-affliction of harboring unforgiveness in their hearts. Accept their apology and let it go. Ask God to help you in forgiving them, and you will find out through his strength that it is possible to forgive. When you forgive, you find yourself walking in obedience to Christ's teachings and the peace of God which surpasses all understanding will guard your hearts and minds.

Today, let the Holy Spirit permeate your heart as you pray this prayer in Matthew 6:9-13, "Our Father in heaven hallowed by your name, your kingdom come, your will be done on earth as in heaven. Give us this day our daily bread. And forgive us our debts, as we forgive our debtors. And do not lead us into temptation. But deliver us from the evil one, for yours is the Kingdom and the power and glory forever, Amen."

HELP WANTED FATHERS, APPLY IN PERSON

Imparting the Blessing of a Great Grandfather to his Great Grandson

I do not know how to start my story or where, but my family was one of the only ones in my neighborhood who had a father and a mother in the home, and I was proud of that, even though they used to fuss and fight. Then one day, my dad came home from work, packed his things and just left and did not come back.

After that, I felt a lot of resentment towards my mother, and I started to live with my grandmother more than I did with my own mother. I know that situation changed me differently than my brothers. I do not think what happened was planned. One day, we packed up and went to see my other relatives. I would hear stories about them as I was growing up, but I never thought that these people were real, because I had never seen them before.

The two and a half hours drive from Moultrie, Georgia to visit them had my mind on high alert. My grandmother was not a big talker, so the whole trip was done in silence. I wondered the whole way how these people were going to be or going to look or talk, because any person who was older than my grandmother, I thought must have been older than dirt. I still could not believe that my grandmother was taking me to see people I always believed were dead.

Once we got there, I was afraid to get out of the car. My grandmother told me that it was alright, and my grandmother was one of the only people at that time that I trusted. I felt better at that time and people came out that looked huge to me… as a matter of fact, everybody that came out looked huge. That is when I found out that my grandmother was the youngest of the other brothers and sisters. This lady ran out and hugged my grandmother really tight.

I thought this lady would break my grandmother, and when she saw me, she asked my grandmother my name. I did not say anything, I just looked at my grandmother and when she nodded, I told the lady that my name was Michael Walker and she just smiled and hugged me. At this time, I had never been hugged by anyone but my grandmother. Then my grandmother's sister said, "I like him." My grandmother told her sister that I was her favorite.

I guessed from the way that they were acting that they had not seen my grandmother in a long time. I was sacred out of my mind, so I hid behind my grandmothers' legs. We stayed about three days, and on the last day, when I woke up to eat breakfast, this old man was at the table when I walked in. He looked at me with blue eyes. Now me, not knowing that he was blind, I ran straight to my grandmother and told her what I had seen. She told me that the man was her daddy.

So, you know, that blew my mind. That my grandmother's daddy was still alive. To me, she was old. I could not even think about his age. He called my grandmother and told her to bring me to him. I just knew I was going to die. When we got in there, he asked my name. I told him, because I was scared. He told me that his name was Elam and he called me over to him. He put his hands on both sides of my head and put his forehead against mine and told me to believe. He told me that I will be alright. I felt good, but I was still scared…just not as much. He told my grandmother that I was going to be alright. We ate breakfast and we stayed a little while longer before leaving.

From that day, it seemed like every adversity I encounter, God has shown me favor, and I believe that it was because of the imparting of blessing my great grandfather imparted upon me. I remember my great grandfather's words, "He'll be alright," and I have been just that. Alright.

Chapter Eleven

The Mothers Role in the Absence of the Father

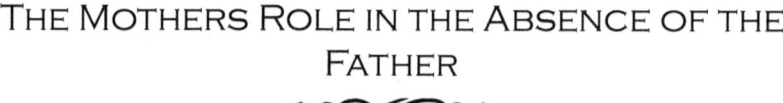

They say that she is the weaker vessel, but if you measure her strength to the physical strength of a man, she would certainly be the weaker vessel. If you measure her strength from within, you will be surprised how much strength she possesses. If it were not for many mothers, many of our families would not have survived. I know fathers are the backbone of the family, but in many families today, our backbone is missing. The weaker vessel had to fill in the gap for the family to survive.

I applaud every mother who never thought whether she was strong enough to fill in the gap when the father was absent from the home. She just stood up and did what was needed to fill in the gap when the father was absent from the home. She did not sit around and ask questions about whether or not she was strong enough to fill in the gap of a MIA father. Many mothers stood up for the challenge, and with God's help, that weaker vessel made it through when the odds were against her.

Where did she get this strength? It came from God and from within. Believe it or not, it was there all the time and most of us men never notice it. It reveals itself when needed and most of those times are in the absence of the father in the home. I have personally seen the strength of my mother in my father's absence. I saw the sacrifices she made just so her children could have food, shelter, and clothing. Like I said before, my mother was the spiritual leadership in our family.

Her faith was ordinary but brough extraordinary results from the God she trusted. As a child, we constantly saw God's favor working in our home because of her faith in a God that he could do all that she asked or thought. I remember times when we would get sick, and she would anoint us with oil and pray over us and we were well. Other times, God would bless her financially, like I said, we constantly saw God's favor in our home in my father's absence. She definitely was not physically stronger than my dad, but she certainly was spiritually strong and through her weakness, God made her strong so she would be able to fill the gap of the absence of a father.

She did not try to take my fathers place, she just stepped up and filled the space of taking care of her family. Somebody had to, or we would have been left in the cold. Have you ever thought about the bond between a mother and her child? For nine months, she carried that fetus, child, inside of her womb. There is a bond between that child and that mother that we cannot explain or understand in it's fulness. She will protect her child no matter what it takes, even if her life is on the line.

We will never know, at least I believe, the fullness of a mother's love and the sacrifices that she makes for her children. A mother's heart is to do whatever she had to do, that is morally right for the survival of her family, even in the father's absence.

The Baby Momma Drama Syndrome

I do not know if you have heard it called by this name or not, but many call it the baby momma drama syndrome. It is when the mother and father do not see eye to eye in their relationship and they usually end up splitting up and getting a divorce. Now, the momma is so full of bitterness and anger that she tries to use the child as a weapon for her advantage against the father by not letting him see or visit his child. She gets mad with him for some reason or another and then puts the child in the middle of all of their drama.

The mother uses the child for her revenge against the father and that revenge is meant to inflict punishment in the form of injury or insult upon her exes. She uses the child in return by not letting them see their father for the injury that he caused her. We call this the "baby momma drama syndrome."

Now, what happens in a lot of these situations is that the child gets hurt because their mother will not let the father see or visit his child. Now the child becomes angry at their mother for keeping them away from their father. Whether the mother knows it or not, that child longs for a relationship with both of his parents, but here we see the mother denies her child the right to have their father in their life.

I wonder how many men out there or how many men are reading this book are going through the baby momma drama syndrome right now. You have tried all you know how to do to be in your child's life, but their mother will not allow it. There are a lot of men in this situation.

Well, mothers, I would like to speak with you for a minute or two concerning your actions in this matter. First, nothing good is going to come from you acting like this. As a matter of fact, it is far worse than anything else that will come from this. I am not saying that you are to blame, as it takes two to tangle. I am not saying that your ex's did not hurt you, but what I am saying is that you must not practice evil for evil, because love conquers evil.

I know that there are two sides to every story. As a matter of fact, there are three sides to every story usually and those are your side, his side, and the truth. That is usually how it goes. One of the worst things that can happen is your child becomes bitter and angry at you for keeping them away from their father. Just imagine one morning, waking up and finding that your child is gone. Where did you think she or he might have gone?

Have you ever thought to be with their dad, whom you tried to keep out of their lives? It is something for you to seriously think about before you turn your own daughter or son against you. Remember that there are always consequences to our actions, remember that what you sow is what you reap. No. I am not one of those men who will say that if I cannot see my children then I am not going to pay child support.

Men, you should always take care of your children, always, and there is no excuse for men not taking care of their children. I do not care if you do not have visitation rights or not, as a man and a father, which is your responsibility. If you truly love your child, you will be glad to do all that you can for your child. Your responsibility is not based on how your ex treats you. I know that you may be thinking she is misusing the funds that you pay each month, but that is not an excuse either. If she is misusing the funds, just know that what is done in secret will come to light or be exposed. You do your part and keep records of all of your payments and it will work out in your favor.

If there is any wrong being done, remember that what goes around comes around. Now, I am not letting men off, remember when I said before that it takes two to tangle. Well, it does. There are some men out there who go around sowing their wild oats and making babies only to not take care of them. We call them dead beat dads. Dead beat dads are men with boys' brains. They are in control by living for the moment, and they are driven by lust.

They come around when it is beneficial to them and then they want the credit for something that someone else did. This usually happens when the child has grown up and become successful. They are the ones who will yell out, "That's my son!" or "That's my daughter," even though they had never brought the child a pamper or a bottle of milk. Dead beat dads are the right name for these guys. We can only hope that one day their brains will catch up with their bodies and then they can man up and handle their responsibilities as fathers.

Until then, lets keep praying for them.

Chapter Twelve

Fathers and Mothers Working for the Betterment of their Children After a Divorce or Separation

When it comes to marriage, no marriage is perfect, and this is because we are not perfect human beings. There are good marriages and there are bad marriages. All marriages will experience trials and hardships. Through the help of God, they can survive and weather the storms of life challenges. Now, what do they do when the marriage does not weather the storms or survive life's challenges? Well, these marriages usually end in divorce, and it hurts the family. It is sad to say, but the children are the ones who usually get hurt the most, because they love their two parents even though those two parents do not love each other anymore.

Now you have two people who were once in love, or lust so they say, and they now cannot even stand each other. Nor can they stand to be in each other's presence, so this makes it so that divorce is their best option, at least, that is what they have considered. Now at their divorce hearing, the judge awards one parent full custody of the children and the other parent visitation rights. Now the children will have to be moved around like a pawn on a chess board from one parent to the other or one parent would have full custody of the children while the other parent has no visitation at all due to a decision that was made by the court for some reason or another which is supposed to be in the best interest of the child.

Best interest of the child…or rather, the best interest of the other, bitter, angry parent who has been given full custody and has been using the child as a weapon to keep that child from their father or mother. It is nothing new and you have seen it before where parents use their children as a weapon to get at their ex. I encourage you as parents to work together for the betterment of your children.

Your children need each of you to be in their lives. They do not want to choose between a mother and father, I would not. They need you in their lives. I plead with you to work out whatever problems you and your ex's have for the future of your children.

I will repeat it again, you have read the statistics earlier in this book. Believe me. Do you want one of these statistics to be one of your children? I believe that you do not and if I am right, then you should put all of your petty differences aside for the betterment of your children. This is your time to put your children's needs above your own personal revenge towards your ex's.

It is time for each of you to act like parents and not like kids. We can expect this kind of behavior from kids, but it should never be expected, seen, or accepted in adults.

The Workaholic Parents, Too Busy for their Children

My story may differ from some of the others that you may have read. My name is Jason. I came from a home where both my father and my mother were there. As a matter of fact, they have been happily married now for 45 years.

They worked so hard when I was younger to provide a good home and a good life for me, but they were never home. My father was a truck driver-owner operator and my mother worked at a Big Bank. They would leave early in the morning and get home late at night. I know that their intended well, but I just wanted to spend some time with them and that rarely happened.

Do not get me wrong. I had the best of the best, but I would have given it all up just to have them spend some family time together with me. My grandparents spent more time with me than my own parents did, due to them working all the time. When I reached the age of 14 years old, I thought I was grown, and I left home and then life went crazy.

I was living on the streets of New York City and I was introduced to drugs and some bad ways of life, but through the Grace of God, I never got caught until later on in my life, that is, until my luck ran out, and by that, I mean that one must never take Grace and the mercy of God for granted. He blessed me with a wonderful woman who would later on become my wife. We had four children, two girls and two boys.

Oh yeah, time for daddy to go to work. Well, long story short, I went to work alright. I started around 5:00am and sometimes leave the shop 10:00-11:00pm or come home for 30 minutes to an hour for lunch and supper and then be back to work. I remember my kids begging me to play with them and I would tell them, "I will tomorrow." The sad thing is that tomorrow would never come.

Eventually, bills were bigger, and we needed more money. This is when I was introduced to the ways of making methamphetamine and boy the money was coming in left and right. Then, God's grace and mercy that I was taking for granted came to a screeching halt and I found myself behind prison bars with a six-year sentence. My wife left me, I lost my job and everything else except God. Now what bothers me the most is not being able to be around my kids.

I think of all the times I could have spent with them, but I felt I had to work. I was repeating the same workaholic behaviors as my parents and did not even realize it. I have lost so much time with my kids that I can never get back, and all because I was so busy working. My prayer today is that God give me another opportunity to be reconciled with them, and believe me, I would spend more time with them this time around. I learned my lesson the hard way.

I also hope and pray some of you will learn from my mistakes and do not take your kids for granted nor the Grace of God that he has given you.

The Resolution For the Absence of Fathers in the Home

Today, we must come up with a resolution which is a course of action determined or decided on to get fathers back in their rightful place, which is in their children's lives. The survival of our children depends on fathers taking action concerning their absence. We gave you the statistics throughout this book on the absence of fathers in their children's lives. What we are seeking now is a course of action to take. We have been talking too long and now it is time to do something about this epidemic of fatherless homes. Yes, I call it an epidemic.

An epidemic is a disease that spread rapidly and extensively by infection and affects many individuals in an area or a population at the same time. Well, the absence of fathers in American homes is spreading rapidly and extensively by affecting our children in many areas of our cities or populations at the same time.

Many families are affected by the absence of fathers. I call this an epidemic and believe me; it is one and it is spreading. We have been taking the absence of fathers in the homes too lightly. It is as serious as the outbreak of a disease. What would you call 63% of youth who commit suicide coming from fatherless homes, or 75% of all adolescent patients in chemical abuse centers coming from fatherless homes?

I call it an epidemic and it is heartbreaking because it affects the lives and the innocence of children. Every time I look at these statistics it lets me know how serious the problem of fatherless homes really is. Tell me this is not an epidemic. We need a resolution, and we need one now. Here are six steps to a resolution that God has placed on my heart:

1. We need to educate fathers on all of the negative statistics and how serious it is for their children to live in fatherless homes, and their future living in such homes. If they know the effects it brings upon their children,

maybe their hearts will be moved to be in their children's lives.
2. Every father that is absent from their child's life should acknowledge that their actions of not being in their child's life was wrong. He must admit his absence for one reason or another. Believe me, there is no excuse, and he must admit his mistakes. He has to come to that point himself. If he continues to justify his wrong actions, he can never see the error of his choice not being in their lives.
3. Act: Every father that is absent in their child's life should begin to take action in repairing their relationship with their child. Whatever it takes he must be willing to do for the survival of his child, but know this, nothing can ever be done until he tries. "The time is always right to do what is right," (Martin Luter King Jr.).
4. Take it slow: Rome was not built in a day. Trust has to be earned and you need to prove yourself to be accepted as their father. They cannot afford to be hurt again. Remember the broken promises that you made before and remind yourself to take it slow.
5. Be patient: Do not look for their approval quickly, and they are not going to just let you walk into their lives that easy. It takes time for wounds to heal. Remember you made the choice to not be in their life even though they always wanted you. Just think if it was you in their place.
6. Pray: I know you may not be religious, but believe me, you will never know the power of prayer until you pray, with faith. You will need the help of the creator in reconciliation with your child, and you must have faith that he will intervene on your behalf.

I believe these six steps of resolutions will help you reconcile with your child if it is done with the right motive and from the heart. Remember that we are in this together and everyone deserves another chance.

I am believing and praying for your reconciliation with your child.

Closing Remarks by the Author:

Min. Warren Baker Sr.

Today, the epidemic of fatherless homes is serious, very serious. Please do not take this epidemic lightly. Our children's lives are at stake. I have personally given you my own testimony of God restoring me with my sons. Believe me, it was not me. It was God working things on my behalf and all because I acknowledged my mistakes and then repented of those mistakes.

My sons suffered a lot because of me not being in their lives. Your sons and daughters have suffered because of you not being in their lives. This must stop and it must stop right now as I speak. I plead with you to repair the damage that your absence has caused in your children's lives. I do not have a son behind these prison walls, but some of you do, and believe me…even behind these prison walls the cry can be heard echoing from the absence of their fathers.

I talk to many of these young men every day and many of them say the same thing over and over again, "I didn't have a father in my life, I wish I did." With some of you, it has been a long time since you have spoken to your children. It is time to break the ice and be reconciled with your children.

Ask God to intervene on your behalf while you pursue a relationship with your children and watch God give you the breakthrough of your life. I believe in you, but most of all, I believe in God, and He is a God of another chance.

Thumb's up my brothers.

www.ingramcontent.com/pod-product-compliance
Lightning Source LLC
Chambersburg PA
CBHW071910070526
44583CB00016B/1925